AMERICAN HORTICULTURAL SOCIETY
PRACTICAL GUIDES

ROSES

AMERICAN HORTICULTURAL SOCIETY
PRACTICAL GUIDES

ROSES

LINDEN HAWTHORNE

DK PUBLISHING, INC.
www.dk.com.

A DK PUBLISHING BOOK
www.dk.com

PRODUCED FOR DORLING KINDERSLEY BY PAGE*One*,
Cairn House, Elgiva Lane, Chesham, Buckinghamshire
PROJECT EDITOR Charlotte Stock
PROJECT DESIGNER Suzanne Tuhrim

SERIES EDITOR Pamela Brown
SERIES ART EDITOR Stephen Josland
MANAGING EDITOR Louise Abbott
MANAGING ART EDITOR Lee Griffiths
US EDITOR Ray Rogers

PRODUCTION Ruth Charlton, Mandy Innes

First American Edition, 1999
2 4 6 8 10 9 7 5 3 1

Published in the United States by DK Publishing, Inc.
95 Madison Avenue, New York, New York 10016

Library of Congress Cataloging-in-Publication Data

Roses
        p. cm. — (AHS practical guides)
    Includes index.
    ISBN 0–7894–4155–1 (alk. paper)
    1. Rose culture. 2. Roses. I. DK Publishing, Inc. II. Series.
    SB411.R715 1999
    635.9'33734—dc21   98–48213
                                                CIP

Reproduced by Colourscan, Singapore
Printed and bound by Star Standard Industries, Singapore

CONTENTS

ROSES IN THE GARDEN 7

An introduction to the many ways in which roses can be grown in the garden, and the different flower forms, habits, uses, and characteristics of the main rose groups.

CARING FOR YOUR ROSES 29

Choosing, planting, and training roses; how and when to prune the different types; how to encourage better blooms, and how to keep plants healthy.

A GALLERY OF ROSES 53

A photographic guide to roses of all kinds.

ROSES IN THE GARDEN

WHAT ARE ROSES?

THE MOST ROMANTIC AND MOST ENDURING of all garden plants, roses have been displayed probably since gardens were first cultivated. They have certainly been grown for many centuries, prized not only for the ornamental beauty of their exquisite, often supremely fragrant flowers, but also for hips, leaves, and roots used for medicinal purposes and, of course, for their scented oils – attar of roses is still used to lend distinctly feminine notes to modern perfumes. Roses are, quite simply, indispensable in today's gardens.

THE ROSE FAMILY

The genus *Rosa*, one of the largest in the plant family Rosaceae, consists of about 150 species of deciduous and semi-evergreen shrubs, climbers, and ramblers. Driven by the enthusiasm for roses, plant breeders have created thousands of cultivars. A few of the roses grown today existed in pre-Roman times and would have been easily identifiable in medieval monastery gardens, but the majority were developed from the mid-1700s onward. Breeding programs continue unabated and, each year, new roses of almost every size and type are introduced, to scent and decorate even the smallest of modern plots.

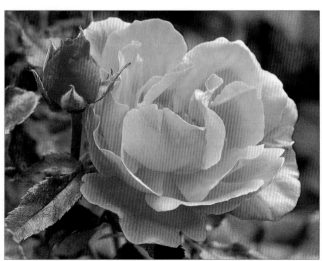

FRAGRANCE AND BEAUTY
A modern rose, the floribunda Fragrant Delight *combines classic beauty with delicious perfume, both of which can be enjoyed throughout summer.*

◀ ROSE SHOWER *A garden path beneath a tunnel of roses is showered with color and perfume.*

WHY GROW ROSES?

Few gardens, regardless of their scale
or style, fail to benefit from the addition
of a rose. Once you learn more about
roses and grow to love them, just one or
two will seldom be enough to satisfy you.

Roses come in such diverse forms that
their uses in gardens are limited only by
the imagination. The traditional treatment
of hybrid teas and floribundas (large- and
cluster-flowered bush roses) as bedding
plants is the simplest way of using them –
their upright habit is well suited to formal
plantings. However, their versatility as
a group extends beyond being displayed
in flower beds devoted solely to roses.

Shrub roses, both ancient and modern
types, are ideal in mixed borders. They
associate particularly well with other

COOL ELEGANCE
Iceberg *is ideal as a specimen or for
low hedging. Its graceful habit and clusters
of creamy white flowers complement this
mixed planting in shades of silver and blue.*

fragrant shrubs such as *Philadelphus* (mock
orange) and with summer-flowering bulbs
and perennials. Those that are remontant

Shrub roses enhance mixed borders of summer bulbs and perennials

---

(repeat-flowering), whether grown alone
as specimens or in mixed plantings, will
provide glorious color all summer.

SPECIAL INTEREST

Among more recent developments are roses
that are ideal as groundcover. These dense,
small-leaved shrubs effectively block out
the light beneath them and can make good
weed suppressors. Trailing groundcover
roses are ideal for clothing sunny banks,
cascading over terrace walls, or even for
growing in containers. For the smallest
gardens, choose the relatively new patio
or miniature roses, which are tremendous

◀ TRADITIONAL
ROSE GARDEN
*Obelisks joined by
fragrant swags of
roses grown on ropes
rise above a long-
flowering carpet
of floribundas and
hybrid teas, giving
color and fragrance
all summer long.*

▼ ROSY MANTLE
*The bare trunk of
this large tree has
been cloaked by
the repeat-flowering*
Compassion, *which
suits small gardens.*

value within a limited space. They provide
a tailor-made solution for the tiniest of city
gardens and can be grown in containers
or in open ground, in borders or raised
beds. For an added dimension, choose
miniature climbers to fill a vertical space.

Let trailing groundcover roses cascade from hanging baskets

Climbing roses are perfect for clothing
drab or unsightly structures, or for
enhancing large expanses of wall, both
high and low. They can also be trained
on pillars and other ornamental structures
such as pyramids or tepees to give height
and interest to a garden design. When
trained to form a fragrant arbor, they
can provide a place to pause. The more
rampant ramblers are seen at their best
cascading from the limbs of large trees,
with their stems wreathed in blooms.

 All that most roses ask is sun, fertile
weed-free soil, and adequate moisture,
and nutrients; in return, they give great
pleasure over many summer months.

TYPES OF ROSE

Unlike a botanical classification, which groups plants on the basis of similarities and differences between the form, number, and arrangements of flower parts, a horticultural system classifies roses according to their size, habit, and flower form, each group of roses being suited to specific garden purposes. The system presented here is not the same as that used in other parts of the world, but it is the system in most common usage in much of North America.

BUSH AND SHRUB ROSES

With the exception of ramblers and climbers, all roses are classified as shrubs or bushes. A shrub rose is more than 4ft/1.2m tall when fully grown; it often has a more natural, arching habit than bushes and may flower just once or repeatedly. Shrub roses are suitable as single specimens or in mixed plantings in a shrubbery or mixed border. In contrast, bush roses are

DAVID AUSTIN'S ROSES
The so-called English Roses are shrub roses that were bred to combine repeat-flowering qualities of the hybrid teas and floribundas with the flower forms, colors, and fragrances associated with old garden roses.

pruned to a neat, more or less symmetrical form and seldom grow taller than 4ft/1.2m. Nearly all bush roses are repeat-flowering, often over very long periods. They are more useful than shrubs in confined spaces and look good displayed in formal group plantings such as borders and bedding.

CLIMBERS AND RAMBLERS

Most climbers are repeat-flowering roses, bearing flowers on short shoots that arise from old wood and then on new wood later in the season. They are more stiffly upright in habit than the long flexible-stemmed ramblers, most of which produce clusters of flowers only once on growth made during the previous season.

FLOWER FORMS

The relatively simple flower forms of the species roses have been modified by ongoing selection and breeding to yield a number of quite distinct forms (*see below*). Rose flowers range from single (up to 8 petals) and semidouble (8–14 petals) to double (20 or more petals) and fully double (more than 30 petals). They are borne singly or in small or large clusters (corymbs), and they may be once- or repeat-flowering. The continuity of flowering varies according to cultivar and on how well an individual plant has been fed. Its performance can also be affected by the hours of warmth and sunshine in any given season. Some roses flower almost continuously, others bear repeated flushes, and some produce a main flush in early or midsummer, which is followed by a second, lesser flush later in the season.

The scent of roses also varies in intensity to a surprising degree; a few have little if any scent, but those that are fragrant may present exotic notes of anise, myrrh, apples, and other fruity scents as well as the warm, attar of roses fragrance found in old garden roses, such as the damasks.

ROSE FLOWER FORMS

FLAT
Usually single, with one set of petals that open flat to display a boss of stamens at the center. Typically seen in species roses, such as *R. glauca* (*see p.52*).

ROUNDED
Double or fully double flowers with even-sized, overlapping petals forming a bowl-shaped or rounded form, as seen in Tequila Sunrise (*see p.55*).

CUPPED
Open, single to fully double blooms with petals curving upward and outward to cup a central boss of stamens, for example 'New Dawn'. (*see p.68*).

ROSETTE
Almost flat, double or fully double flowers packed with small, overlapping, slightly uneven petals, as seen in 'Great Maiden's Blush' (*see p.62*).

HIGH-CENTERED
Semi- to fully double flowers with petals that rise to form a high-centered point. Seen in hybrid teas, such as Paul Shirville (*see p.53*).

QUARTERED-ROSETTE
Almost flat, double or fully double flowers arranged into four distinct "quarters," for example 'Duc de Guiche' (*see p.64*).

URN-SHAPED
Semi- to fully double, inner petals curving to an urn shape amid flat outer petals. In hybrid teas and floribundas, such as 'Hula Girl' (*see p.58*).

POMPON
Small, rounded, double to fully double flowers, usually in clusters, with masses of small petals. Commonly seen in miniature roses, such as 'White Pet' (*see p.58*).

BUSH ROSES

MOST BUSH ROSES are modern roses, that is, developed since 1867, chiefly by breeders in Europe, the United States, and Australia. Early breeders focused mainly on flower form and color but, in recent years, more attention has been given to improving health, hardiness, and disease resistance; many modern roses, especially those in the *Gallery of Roses* (*see pp.53–61*), have all of these attributes. Bush roses can be further subdivided into distinct groups.

HYBRID TEAS

This group is also referred to as large-flowered bush roses. The first hybrid teas were bred from crosses between hybrid perpetuals and tea roses, which originated in China. From the former, they inherited hardiness and vigor along with large, fragrant flowers which boasted a variety of rich colors. The tea roses bequeathed a reliably repeat-flowering habit, glossy, green leaves, and the high-pointed flower buds that remain beloved by many.

Modern hybrid teas are freely branching, usually thorny-stemmed shrubs of more or less upright or bushy habit. They bear matte or glossy, mid- to dark green leaves composed of quite large oval or lance-shaped leaflets, often flushed with red or purple when young. Their large flowers, mostly urn-shaped or high-centered, are often fragrant and are borne singly or

---

The repeat-flowering habit of hybrid teas was a revolution for growers

---

in clusters of up to three. Since they bear flowers on shoots arising from old wood and, more freely, on new wood, they are usually pruned hard annually (*see p.38*).

▶ CLUSTERS OF COLOR
A typical floribunda,
Valentine Heart *is noted
for its pale pink petals with
slightly frilled margins.*

▼ SINGLED OUT
Remember Me *is a
hybrid tea with high-centered
blooms of rich copper-orange.*

FLORIBUNDAS

Floribundas, or cluster-flowered bush roses, were bred in Denmark at the start of the 20th century. Initially called hybrid polyanthas, they are derived from crossing hybrid tea roses with polyantha roses to produce tough and very floriferous plants.

Floribunda roses provide continuous summer color

In general, floribunda roses have an upright, free-branching habit and need only light pruning (*see p.39*). They are often hardier and healthier than hybrid teas and show greater resistance to disease. Their single or fully double flowers, which are usually smaller and borne in either large clusters or sprays of up to 25 on both the current season's and last year's stems, make them suitable for use in group plantings of nonstop solid color.

PEACHES 'N' CREAM
A display of Just Joey's *large, sweetly fragrant flowers of coppery pink and buff is interspersed with the dainty flowers of flowering tobacco* (Nicotiana).

UNDERPLANTING ROSES

Although bush roses are traditionally seen with bare soil at their base, they can be underplanted with shallow-rooting perennials (*see below*). Leave the immediate root zone free for routine feeding and mulching.
Catmint (*Nepeta* x *faassenii*) Silver leaves and lavender-blue flowers.
Clematis C. *heracleifolia* 'Wyvale', C. *recta*.
Dianthus Clove-scented pinks combine well with rose scents and colors, especially 'Becky Robinson', pink and ruby-red laced; 'Bovey Belle', deep pink; 'Doris', warm pink; and 'Haytor White', white.
Geraniums Many, especially 'A.T. Johnson', 'Graveteye', and 'Mrs Kendall Clark'.
Lavenders 'Munstead' and 'Hidcote'.
Stachys byzantina Silver-leaved groundcover.
Violas Especially soft blues, violets and purples, such as 'Nellie Britton', 'Huntercombe Purple', and 'Prince Henry'.

PATIO AND MINIATURE ROSES

The recent development of patio and miniature roses has helped resolve the problem of finding roses that suit small areas. Patio roses are scaled-down versions of floribundas (cluster-flowered bushes); indeed, their alternative name, dwarf cluster-flowered bush, is often preferred by many growers, since it avoids the implication that they are limited to patio plantings. Patio roses are characterized by compact growth of dense habit and smaller leaves than large floribundas. Few of them are noted for having any scent, but they are valued for their clusters of 3–11 small, single to double flowers that appear reliably in repeated flushes from summer to autumn. Like other small bush roses, they require relatively low maintenance: they do not need the very fertile soil demanded by large roses, and pruning (*see p.40*) amounts to little more than deadheading, along with routine removal of dead wood and thinning if the plants become congested.

> # Of all the roses, miniatures are the easiest to manage in containers

Members of the miniature group are the smallest of all roses, often less than 14in/35cm in height. Raised from the exquisite China rose *R.* 'Rouletii', they are tiny – but perfectly formed – in all their parts and flower throughout summer. They bring a splash of color to even the smallest area, whether grown in containers or used as low hedging or as border edging.

▶ COUNTY ROSE
Cambridgeshire *belongs to the popular series of groundcover roses known as the County Roses, which are named after English shires.*

▼ PERFECT FIT
At 6–10in/15–25cm tall, the miniature rose Bush Baby *is able to make itself at home in the smallest of beds and borders, where it makes excellent edging.*

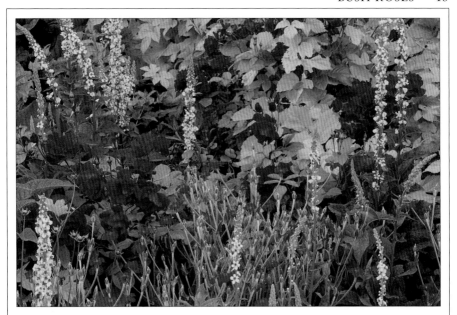

GROUNDCOVER ROSES

With prickly stems and small leaves, groundcover bush or shrub roses provide effective groundcover by virtue of their very dense habit that excludes light from the soil surface, thereby inhibiting germination of weed seedlings. This does not eliminate the need to carry out pre-planting weed clearance and post-planting mulching (*see pp.34–5*) for truly effective groundcover. These routines are absolutely vital and worth carrying out, especially since weeding by hand beneath such prickly bushes can prove a painful task.

STRIKING DISPLAY
A bold planting of pinks and yellows is enhanced by the crimson-scarlet blooms of the patio rose Festival, *which have paler undersides and random streaks of white.*

Groundcover roses adopt one of two growth habits; some are spreading bushes while others are trailing, usually with flower clusters wreathing the entire length of their stems. A few flower once only in summer, but most repeat reliably. They can be used for low bedding and edging but are seen at their best cascading over low walls and banks or the sides of containers.

ROSES FOR CONTAINERS

HOT ORANGES	BRIGHT WHITES	FIERY REDS	PRETTY PINKS
Anna Ford Patio (*p.58*)	**Kent** Groundcover (*p.60*)	**Boy's Brigade** Patio (*p.59*)	**Avon** Blush pink to pearly white, groundcover
Orange Sunblaze Miniature (*p.59*)	**Snowball** Bright creamy white miniature rose	**Festival** Patio (*p.59*)	**Little Bo-peep** Patio (*p.58*)
Shine On Orange-pink patio rose	**Swany** Groundcover (*p.60*)	**'Fire Princess'** miniature (*p.59*)	**'Nozomi'** Ground-cover (*p.61*)
Sunseeker Orange-red with yellow eye, patio rose	**'White Pet'** Patio (*p.58*)	**Red Ace** Crimson miniature rose	**Queen Mother** Patio (*p.58*)
		Robin Redbreast Patio (*p.58*)	

SHRUB ROSES

THE TERM SHRUB ROSE is a catchall for large, relatively modern roses that do not fall neatly into other categories, from the hybrid musks developed at the start of the 20th century to new types of English rose. Although most, by definition, are taller than 4ft/1.2m, they are a diverse group. Habit ranges from upright to gracefully arching, and they bear mostly scented, single to fully double flowers, singly or in clusters, usually repeatedly through summer.

HEDGES AND SPECIMENS

The height, spread, and prickly habit make shrub roses perfect for hedging. Best of all are the dense and thorny rugosa roses, with wrinkled, bright green leaves. Their scented, single or semidouble flowers are produced repeatedly through summer, the later blooms borne at the same time as glowing red, tomato-like hips. Few other hedging plants offer such a long season. They need little maintenance: apply balanced fertilizer in spring and lightly trim to shape each year: in early spring for repeat-flowerers, or after flowering for once-flowering cultivars. If positioned in a prominent site that can be viewed from several angles, modern shrubs make good single specimens. These roses

> The tangle of thorny
> stems make rose hedges
> difficult to penetrate

are not hard to cultivate and relatively problem-free, and you are likely to find it difficult to restrict your choice to just one!

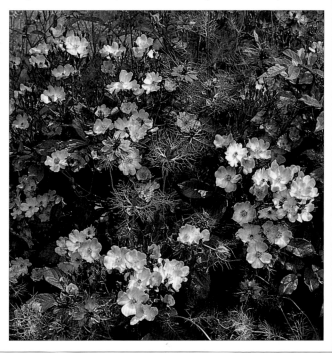

INFORMAL SCREEN
Interspersed with
love-in-a-mist (Nigella
damascena), *the*
dense, spreading
stems and pale pink,
mop-headed flower
clusters of 'Ballerina'
make a colorful
low hedge.

▲ CLIMBING HIGH
*Ideal for training against
a wall, the fruit-scented*
Abraham Darby *has a
vigorous bushy habit and
may grow up to 5ft/1.5m tall.*

◄ SHADES OF GREEN
The grayish green leaves of
L.D. Braithwaite *offer foliage
interest in a mixed border,
while the fragrant crimson
flowers add strong color.*

MIXED BORDERS

Shrub roses are rivaled only by old garden roses (*see pp.18–9*) for planting in mixed borders – and many have the advantage of blooming repeatedly through summer, instead of in a single flush. The modern shrubs known as "English roses," bred by David Austin, provide the best features of both. By crossing modern hybrid teas and floribundas with selected old garden roses, they offer repeat flowering with the flower form, color, habit, and much-loved scents of old garden roses.

 In general, shrub roses are more suited to mixed plantings among shrubs, bulbs, or perennials than are other rose groups. This is partly because their shrubby habit makes them more graceful than the rigid, upright bush roses and partly because of their range of colors, softer than the startling, almost fluorescent hues found in other modern roses. Shrub roses have sufficient stature to form a backdrop for low-growing plants and hold their own with other medium-sized or large shrubs. Many of them demand a good, fertile soil for maximum performance. This can be achieved by an annual or twice-yearly feeding and a mulch of well-rotted manure (*see pp.34–5*). Most shrub roses need little pruning (*see p.42*) other than to shorten main stems by one-third of their length when dormant or after flowering.

GOOD COMBINATIONS

'Buff Beauty' Apricot then buff, with deep blue *Geranium himalayense* 'Graveteye'.

Gertrude Jekyll Deep pink. The blooms complement the blue-flowered herbaceous *Clematis heracleifolia* 'Wyvale'.

Graham Thomas Rich yellow, with orange-red *Phygelius capensis*, and yellow-flowered *Viola* 'Irish Molly' beneath.

'Penelope' The pale creamy pink blooms go well with the blue-flowered *Campanula lactiflora* 'Prichard's Variety'.

OLD GARDEN ROSES

THIS GROUP INCLUDES some of the most ancient roses known in cultivation – the albas, gallicas, damasks, centifolias, and mosses – which are of European origin and, with rare exceptions, bloom only once in spring or summer. The group also includes hybrids between European and Oriental roses, such as the Chinas, teas, Bourbons, and Portlands, which feature similar characteristics to the old European roses but bloom repeatedly in summer.

WHY GROW OLD ROSES?

While you may at first think that the once-flowering habit of old roses is a major drawback, as you become more familiar with this group it will seem mean-spirited to fault a plant for having only a single, albeit profuse, flush of blooms. If, however, you are resolved to have a nonstop display of flowers throughout summer, choose from the remontant types such as Bourbon and Portland roses. The early crosses of Chinese and European roses yielded repeat-flowering offspring with much of the grace and fine color of the older roses. In the 19th century, they captured breeders' imaginations to such an extent that they became the springboard for the development of modern hybrid teas.

There are old roses to suit almost every purpose: beds and borders – especially mixed borders; walls, fences, and pillars; and for more adventurous, training on pyramids, arbors, or other structures (*see pp.46–7*). They have, for the most

▶ SPILLING OVER
*An informal hedge of
'Complicata' would
suit a naturalistic
setting or wildflower
garden. Its cascading
flowers are attractive
to honeybees.*

▼ JACOBITE ROSE
*The bright creamy
white blooms of
R. x alba 'Alba
Maxima' relieve the
dull gray backdrop
of a drab wall.*

▲ SOFT FOCUS
*The colored foliage of
purple sage enhances
a solitary, clear pink
bloom of* Fantin-Latour.

◄ RIPPLED ROSES
*Also known as Rosa Mundi,
R. gallica 'Versicolor' is ideal
for mixed borders. Here, its
striped flowers associate with
pink geraniums to make a
vibrant display.*

part, a graceful, natural habit and often flower so freely that stems bend under the weight. The majority are vigorous, tough, and very hardy, many having been in cultivation for more than 150 years.

Old roses are tough and vigorous and need minimal care

Although most old roses will thrive on minimal attention, they richly reward a little extra feeding with fertilizer and organic mulches. Some may prove slightly prone to mildew but are generally healthy.
  The flowers range from single to fully double, and some are so crammed with petals that they are packed into "quarters." They unfurl to reveal the purest of shades, from soft, clear pink to sumptuous crimson and deepest, velvety maroon-purple. Unlike the more color-fast modern roses, the dark-colored old roses fade with good

grace, revealing hues and tints of lilac, lavender, violet, and mauve. As for their fragrances, they are simply the true rose scents against which all others must be measured. From spicy perfumes and heady musks to delicate hints of fresh apples and citrus fruits, the intoxicating aromas of old garden roses provide the perfect excuse to linger in their presence.

RECOMMENDED

FLOWERS	FRAGRANCE
'Boule de Neige' Bourbon (*p.62*)	**'Belle de Crécy'** Deep cerise-pink gallica with intense spicy scent
'Cardinal de Richelieu' Dark velvety purple gallica	**'Bourbon Queen'** Bourbon (*p.63*)
'Duc de Guiche' Gallica (*p.64*)	**R. x centifolia 'Muscosa'** (*p.63*)
'Empereur du Maroc' Hybrid perpetual (*p.64*)	**'Great Maiden's Blush'** Alba (*p.62*)
'Madame Hardy' White damask	**'Reine des Violettes'** Hybrid perpetual (*p.64*)

FOLIAGE, HIPS, AND THORNS

W HILE HYBRID ROSES OF ALL KINDS are grown and valued primarily for their blooms and long flowering season, it is easy to overlook a number of other sterling garden virtues. The wild or species roses, in particular, along with selections and simple hybrids derived from them, offer beautifully delicate flowers but, in addition, may also have brilliantly colored, often large or unusually shaped hips as well as attractive foliage or spectacular thorny stems.

SPECIES ROSES

Natives of prairies and woodland, species roses possess a beauty of quite a different order to that of their highly bred garden cousins. They are admired for their elegantly natural habit of growth, their small-leaved foliage, and the simplicity of their mostly single flowers. Species roses meld perfectly into informal or naturalistic plantings, in a wildflower garden, or mixed informal hedge. Their ornamental hips also make a splash of color during autumn and provide a welcome source of food for birds in winter. Climbing species roses are seen at their best when doing what comes naturally to them, scrambling up trees and tumbling down in cascades. Wild roses are quite self-sufficient and require little attention. Other than keeping old plants

---

Species roses are ideal for mixed hedges or woodland plantings

---

clear of accumulations of dead wood, they need little in the way of pruning – indeed, minimal pruning is recommended to preserve their natural grace and form.

▲ INCENSE ROSE
The primrose-scented
R. primula has dainty leaves
and a strikingly simple flower.

▶ FIERY FRUITS
The glossy red hips of
Schneezwerg, a rugosa rose,
provide decorative interest
from late summer to autumn.

▲ JAGGED EDGE
R. sericea *f.*
pteracantha *displays
its winged, blood-red
thorns to best
effect in sunlight.*

◄ DOG ROSE
*Sometimes seen
along roadsides,*
R. canina *is ideal
for large plantings.*

ORNAMENTAL VALUE

The flowers of wild roses are nearly always single and most flower once only, often early in the season, as with the incense-scented flowers of *R. primula,* which appear in late spring. Many of them have a high nectar content, making them very attractive to bees, and possess distinctive scents, such as the clove-scented flowers of *R. paulii* or the musk-scented *R. moschata.* In cool, damp conditions and after rain, the leaves of *R. rubiginosa* emit an applelike fragrance that permeates the air for some distance. This characteristic appears in all its hybrid offspring, the sweet briars, making them a perfect addition to informal hedges or boundary plantings. Some wild roses are among the higher ranks of foliage shrubs: *R. pimpinellifolia* and its offspring boast daintily fernlike leaves, and *R. glauca* is admired for its beautiful gray-mauve leaves, borne on red-purple stems. The many different hips also add to the ornamental value of wild roses and prolong their season of interest. They range from the bristly yellow-green fruits of the chestnut rose, *R. roxburghii,* to the scarlet flasks of *R. moyesii* and the glossy black hips of the Scots rose, *R. pimpinellifolia.*

GOOD COMBINATIONS

R. glauca *(p.52)* works well with the red-leaved smoke bush, *Cotinus coggygria* 'Royal Purple', and the cream flowers of *Clematis* 'Henryi'. It also looks very effective with the *Clematis* 'Etoile Violette'.

R. x richardii with the creamy yellow flowers of *Clematis* 'Guernsey Cream'.

R. rubiginosa *(p.63)* woven in hedging with fragrant-leaved roses 'Amy Robsart', 'Anne of Geierstein', and 'Lady Penzance', and the midblue *Clematis alpina* 'Frances Rivis'.

CLIMBERS AND RAMBLERS

WHETHER SCALING WALLS or grown over arches, arbors, pergolas, or pillars, climbers and ramblers are invaluable for adding a vertical dimension to your plantings. The difference in their habits makes each of them better suited to certain uses in the garden; climbers are distinguished by their stiff upright growth, which enables them to grow well against walls, while the flexible stems of ramblers make them easier to train over pergolas, pyramids, and arches.

ADAPTABLE CLIMBERS

Climbing roses produce large, usually scented blooms, singly or in small clusters. They branch freely to form a rigid, woody framework, bearing flowers on new growth at the stem tips but mostly on sideshoots from old wood. You can encourage this habit by training stems to the horizontal when still young and flexible. If given their way, climbers bloom freely at the top of the plant, but if the stems are trained sideways or wound around obelisks or pillars, they create walls and towers of scent and color that last for much of the summer season. Many climbers are equally useful for clothing unsightly garden structures or for softening the strong lines of formal architectural features. The most vigorous can be grown on pergolas, but they need to be tall-growing if they are to produce sufficient length to clothe the top of the structure. Nearly all climbers are less rampant than ramblers.

Miniature climbers, such as 'Laura Ford', rarely exceed 6½ft/2m, are especially useful in tiny gardens and can even be grown in containers. Some, such as 'Mrs. Sam McGredy' or 'Etoile de Hollande', are

ROSE TAPESTRY
A reliable and versatile favorite that tolerates poor soils, 'Albertine' is grown here as a sprawling shrub, with clematis scrambling through. It produces clusters of fragrant, soft salmon-pink flowers over many weeks in summer.

STANDING PROUD
'Rosy Mantle' *displays the typical stiffly upright habit of climbing roses. A neat, fragrant rose, it is well suited to training on walls in small gardens.*

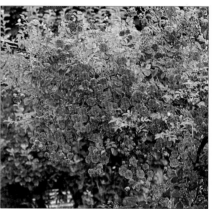

ROSE SHOWERS
The long, flexible stems of 'Dorothy Perkins', *bearing dense trusses of double flowers, are typical of rambling roses and are best displayed spilling down from tall structures.*

climbing sports (mutations caused by a change in their genetic makeup) of hybrid tea roses. They are often healthier and more vigorous than their parents and in many cases have overtaken them in popularity.

Climbers are stiffly upright, while ramblers have scrambling stems

ACCOMMODATING HABITS
Ramblers are rampant growers, with long, flexible stems that grow from the base of the plant. They tend to produce many small flowers, often in spectacularly large sprays, and most bloom only once on year-old wood in early to midsummer. A few, such as 'Sanders' White Rambler' and 'Dorothy Perkins', bloom usefully late in the season when most other once-blooming roses are past their best.

The flexible stems of ramblers are trained easily onto pyramids, pergolas, and swags of rope, which all permit free air circulation. Ramblers are a little more prone than climbers to mildew, which thrives in warm, stagnant air; if wall-grown, provide a support that is set away from the wall. The most rampant, such as 'Bobbie James' or 'Seagull', are better scrambling through strong, healthy trees to form a cascade of bloom from their branches. When choosing a rose for this purpose, it is essential that you match the vigor of the rose to that of the host tree, since the considerable weight of a mature rambler is quite capable of pulling over a small or weak tree.

GOOD COMBINATIONS

'Albertine' (rambler) with blue-flowered purple sage, *Salvia officinalis* Purpurascens, and *Linaria* 'Canon Went'.

'Climbing Iceberg' (climber) with *Clematis* 'Marie Boisselot', both pure white.

'Félicité Perpétue' (rambler) with *Clematis* 'Huldine', *Fuchsia magellanica* var. *molinae*, and *Anemone hupehensis* for a delicate pink and white combination.

'Gloire de Dijon' (climber) with fragrant, creamy apricot buff blooms, and *Clematis* 'Polish Spirit', rich purple-blue.

Handel (climber), cream with magenta-pink petal margins, and the white-flowered *Clematis* 'Duchess of Edinburgh'.

WALLS, PILLARS, AND PERGOLAS

To these may also be added arches, arbors, obelisks, tripods, and a whole range of trelliswork as well as existing structures that may need to be brightened with color or disguised by bushy growth. Whatever the structure, it can be used to provide a focal point in a design or strong vertical elements to a planting design. The special training required for roses allows you to display their particular flower forms with impressive effects.

ROSES ON WALLS

Wall-training is nearly always associated with climbers or ramblers, but there are many roses with long flexible stems that enjoy the warmth and thrive best on a wall. Constance Spry, a sprawling, ungainly shrub when freestanding, displays its huge, myrrh-scented soft pink flowers to fabulous effect if trained on a warm-toned wall.

A backdrop of brick or stone can form an attractive foil for rose flowers, but it also has incidental benefits. The reflected warmth of the sun aids the maturation of wood which, in turn, improves the flowering, as mature wood always flowers more freely. Where the opportunity exists for special training, you are presented with the chance to further increase the flowering potential of a rose. Leading shoots grow relentlessly upward under the control of hormones, which flow back from the topmost bud to suppress branching. If a stem is bent to the horizontal and tied in, the flow of hormones is reduced and sideshoots branch out. In roses, it is these sideshoots that bear the most flowers.

ROSE-TRAINED WALL
The soft pink blooms of 'New Dawn'
bring out the warmth of a garden wall.
This is one of the most shade-tolerant roses
and does well on a north- or west-facing wall.

◀ PLACE TO PAUSE
A pergola bearing Compassion *and* 'Aloha' *on its pillars, and* 'Sanders' White Rambler' *on top, makes an attractive focal point in a garden.*

▼ SOARING PILLAR
The trunk of an old apple tree is wreathed in the sprays of white flowers produced by 'Seagull', *a vigorous rambler.*

ADDED DIMENSION

Far from being purely decorative, nearly all three-dimensional structures permit good air movement and so are positively beneficial to the health of a rose. Again, special training of roses on these structures will produce abundant flowers. The stems of 'Seagull' (*see right*) are wound gently upward in a spiral around an old tree stump to produce a magnificent pillar of flowers. Similar effects can be achieved on obelisks or pyramids with climbers, ramblers, or any flexible-stemmed roses.

Winding stems in a gentle upward spiral yields a mass of blooms

For the best results on pergolas, make sure that you choose a rose that is tall enough to produce horizontal growth when it reaches the top of the pillars. This allows the cascades of flowers to be appreciated from below. A spectacular effect is gained by using roses of different vigor to clothe alternate pillars, with the most rampant trained to cover the top.

SPECIAL EFFECTS

WHATEVER THE OVERALL STYLE of your plantings, whether they be formal, informal, or even wild and naturalistic, some of the most stunning and unexpected effects can be created with roses. It just takes a little special training or some lateral thinking to break free from the idea that roses belong only in beds and borders. With such diversity of habit and form, and a vast catalog from which to choose, roses offer enormous scope to the adventurous mind.

CASCADES AND COVER

Groundcover roses with a creeping habit, such as Swany or Pheasant (*see p 60*), display flowers at their best if their stems are allowed to cascade freely. To achieve this, grow them trained as weeping standards (*shown below*), or plant them at the top of a slope or bank, where they will cover the ground, rooting as they go, to create a strong horizontal element.

Groundcover roses are valued as low-maintenance carpets of bloom. Shrubby types such as Hertfordshire or Flower Carpet (*see p.61*) can create a striking effect where they are used to delineate a garden path and soften its edges or to provide gradation in height and color within a rosebed or mixed planting. They are also invaluable for concealing drain covers and other low-level eyesores.

▲ TUMBLING TEARS
The weeping standard form shows trailing groundcover roses at their best. Here, 'Nozomi' produces a shower of pearl-pink blooms.

▶ FLORAL FANFARE
Low hedges are the domain of groundcover and patio roses, softening the line of a path and drawing the eye to the strong focal point of an arch.

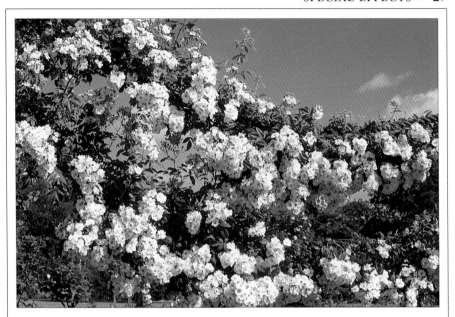

GROWING ON A SWAG
A rampant rambler, 'Rambling Rector' is ideal for training into trees or on ropes, as shown here. It bears huge sprays of white flowers in early summer, followed by red hips in autumn.

LENDING HEIGHT AND GRACE

Roses with flexible stems, such as Graham Thomas and Constance Spry (*see p.65*), are among the most versatile of plants when used to add height to a planting plan. They adapt well to training on vertical structures such as pillars and pergolas, but perhaps the most graceful effects are

> Flowers cascading from a height create graceful effects

achieved when they are grown to display enormous sprays of flowers cascading from a height. This can be done by training roses, preferably vigorous ramblers, along a rope (or chain) suspended between two posts (*see p.47*); double rows of ropes or

chains, often with a rose hedge grown beneath, look particularly good on either side of a garden path. Training roses into trees or large shrubs also creates a colorful cascade of flowers. It makes an attractive feature of fruit trees, such as apple; as the roses bloom after the tree's flowers are over, extending the season of interest. It is essential that you select a less vigorous rambler, such as 'Blush Rambler' (*see p.69*), that will not overwhelm a small host tree.

GOOD COMBINATIONS

Ferdy, a shrubby groundcover rose, makes a low hedge at 30in/75cm; it is covered with pale salmon-pink blooms, that will match those of the clove-scented pink, *Dianthus* 'Doris', used as an underplanting.

White Flower Carpet, groundcover (*p.60*), planted alternately with the purple-flowered lavender *Lavandula* 'Hidcote'.

The blue flowers of *Agapanthus* 'Headbourne Hybrids' with **R. Sussex**, a groundcover rose, forming a 30in/75cm high display of creamy apricot flowers above bronze-green foliage.

'Sanders' White Rambler' (*p.68*) on a swag, matched for vigor with deep purple *Clematis* 'Jackmanii' on the supporting posts.

CARING FOR YOUR ROSES

BUYING AND PLANTING ROSES

WITH ABOUT 150 SPECIES and thousands of rose hybrids and cultivars available, choosing a rose can be a bewildering task. Make sure that you know which type of rose you are selecting so that you can be sure that it is suitable for the intended purpose. Also know whether it flowers only once, repeatedly, or continuously and, most important, how best to prune it.

FINDING THE ROSE YOU WANT

The *Gallery of Roses (see pp.53–69)* contains a good selection of all types of rose. The most enjoyable way of finding more is to visit rose gardens in summer, armed with a notebook. Flower color, form, and fragrance will appeal most immediately, but ask advice too, if you need to, on whether the rose blooms once or repeatedly and whether it is generally healthy. Most garden centers stock a good selection of roses, but if you're unable to find a favorite, contact the American Rose Society, which maintains extensive information files on roses and the details of reputable mail-order suppliers.

ONE ROSE, TWO NAMES
Many roses have two names. Sweet Dream is a trade name for 'Fryminicot', *which is the registered name exclusive to that rose.*

WHAT'S IN A NAME?

Plants are named according to the rules of the International Code of Nomenclature. Names consisting of two words (genus and species) in italics denote a species, for example *Rosa moyesii*. A species name followed by a name in Roman type within single quotes, for example *R. banksiae* 'Lutea', denotes a cultivar (cultivated variety) of a species. An x denotes a simple hybrid that has been cross-bred from two species, e.g. *R. x richardii*.

Roses of complex breeding have just one cultivar name in single quotes, e.g. *R.* 'Agnes'. New introductions are registered by a "code name" to protect the breeder's rights but may be sold internationally by different trade or selling names (*see above*). Naming rules dictate that the first name registered is the true cultivar name, written in single quotes. The trade name is written without single quotes. Both usually appear on the plant label.

◀ HEIGHTENED INTEREST *Within a formal potager,* 'White Pet' *makes a striking standard.*

CHOOSING HEALTHY PLANTS

Ideally, all roses offered for sale are well-grown, correctly labeled, and healthy, but it is always worth running a quick health check on a plant before buying. The soil mix of container-grown roses should be evenly moist and its surface free of mosses and weeds; if choked with weeds, the plant has been in its pot too long and has probably suffered drought or nutrient deficiency. Look for healthy, pale-colored roots in the soil mix, and reject plants whose roots are congested, coiled around the pot, or protruding from the bottom. Plant carefully to give the rose a good start. An application of mulch after planting (*see p.34*) is recommended.

CHOOSING CONTAINER-GROWN ROSES
The specimen on the left has a well-balanced framework of strong shoots clothed with glossy, dark, disease-free leaves and a complement of flower buds almost ready to open. Avoid buying poor specimens that look like the one shown on the right. The plant has long, spindly stems and has suffered from leaf drop, probably as a result of drought, disease, and nutrient deficiency, as seen in the yellowed leaves that are covered in blackspot.

Good number of flower buds

Leaves show signs of disease

Long, spindly stems with sparse foliage

Glossy, healthy-looking foliage

Moist, firm rootball

GOOD SPECIMEN

POOR SPECIMEN

PLANTING CONTAINER-GROWN BUSH ROSES

These can be planted at any time, provided that the soil is not frozen, sodden, or too dry, and that you water well until the rose is established. Dig a hole wide is enough to hold roots without constriction, and deep enough so that the graft union (a visible swelling low down on the main stem) sits level with the soil in USDA Hardiness Zones 6 and 7. Farther north, place the graft union about 1in/2.5cm below the soil level; farther south, the union can sit about 1in/2.5cm above soil level. Fork some organic matter into the bottom, with a handful of bonemeal or slow-release fertilizer. Set the rose in and backfill, firming gently as you go.

Outward-facing bud will produce open growth

Angled cut made ¼in/5mm above bud

PRUNING DORMANT ROSES ON PLANTING
Cut out weak stems to leave 3–5 strong stems. Trim these, making angled cuts to outward-facing buds 3–6in/7–15cm above ground.

BUYING BARE-ROOT ROSES

Bare-root roses are sold and planted during the dormant season. Look for sturdy roots with a complement of fine, fibrous roots, a strong graft union (*see right*), and healthy, well-placed shoots at the top of the plant. Soak the roots in water for an hour before planting. Reject any plants with dried-out roots or sprouting buds; they won't establish well.

Strong graft union, where cultivar joins rootstock

Thick cluster of healthy roots

Weak shoots

Spindly roots

GOOD EXAMPLE
A good set of main roots and fibrous roots support balanced topgrowth.

POOR EXAMPLE
Spindly roots with virtually no system of fibrous roots result in poor topgrowth.

PLANTING BARE-ROOT ROSES

1 **Prune the topgrowth** using clean, sharp pruners to remove any weak, crossing, damaged, or dead shoots. Trim back roots that are damaged to clean, healthy, live roots.

2 **Dig a hole** wide enough to hold the roots unrestricted and deep enough for the graft union to be correctly placed. Fork some well-rotted organic matter into the bottom.

3 **Insert the rose** and check the depth by placing a stake across the hole; the graft union needs to be placed correctly (*see p.30*).

4 **Backfill gently**, making sure roots are in close contact with the soil by firming in as you go. Water in and prune (*see facing page*).

PLANTING AND STAKING STANDARDS

A standard rose is formed by grafting a bush rose (or trailing rose if it is trained as a weeping standard) onto the top of a long, straight stem trained from a vigorous rootstock. The head should have an evenly spaced and well-balanced set of strong shoots growing from a strong graft union. You can usually prune to correct an unbalanced head, but consider buying a poor specimen only if a worthwhile discount is offered on the selling price. The straight stem and union always prove to be the weakest points on a standard rose, and so it will need to be supported by a sturdy stake – one that is long enough to reach the graft union – throughout its life.

1 **Dig a planting hole** as for bare-root roses. Drive in a stake to a depth of 18in/45cm. Place the rose in the hole, checking the depth by placing a stake across the top. The graft union should be placed correctly (*see p.30*). Use the old soil mark on the stem as a guide.

2 **The top of the stake** should reach the graft union, and the stake should be on the side of the prevailing wind. This prevents the plant from leaning into the stake, which would cause chafing of the bark and possibly breakage of the entire head in strong winds.

3 **Attach the rose** to the stake using rose ties with buffers between the stem and the stake. Put one at the top to support the head and one halfway up the stem. Check that they are not too tight, and allow some room for expansion. Cut out weak or crossing shoots.

PLANTING AND TRAINING CLIMBING ROSES

When planting climbers, it is important that you don't cut them back hard, as you do with bush roses. Many are climbing sports (mutations) of bush roses; if pruned too hard, they may revert to a bush habit. In contrast, ramblers naturally produce strong shoots from low down the plant and so need hard pruning upon planting.

This will produce strong new shoots, which can be tied in to the support. Plant both climbers and ramblers 18in/45cm away from their wall or support; this avoids the very dry soil usually found at the base of walls. The shoots can then be guided to the base of the support with ties and stakes, which can be removed later.

Position at angle to avoid dry soil at base of wall

Horizontal wire holds stakes in place

1 For climbers and ramblers, the hole should hold the roots easily when stems are set at an angle of 45°. Check the depth with a stake to make sure that the graft union is placed correctly (*see p.30*).

2 Spread out 4 or 5 of the strongest stems and tie them to stakes pushed into the soil at the base and attached to the lowest wires. Use clips or soft twine for tying in, but check all ties regularly to avoid stem constriction.

WALL-TRAINING AND PRUNING
A CLIMBER IN ITS FIRST SUMMER
The aims of early training are to achieve good coverage by fanning the shoots out so that flowers appear from top to bottom.

3 Tip-prune strong unbranched shoots by 2–3in/5–8cm to encourage sideways-branching sideshoots.

1 Tie in new growth to build a framework, training shoots so they will grow sideways; tie them to wires as they extend.

2 Cut out any spindly, dead, or damaged shoots. Remove original stakes and ties.

ROUTINE CARE

ROSES USE UP considerable energy in producing flowers and replacing growth removed by pruning – that's why they are referred to as "hungry" plants. If you want your roses to grow well and reward you with good-quality flowers all summer long, you need to keep them well fed and healthy. Before you plant, bear in mind that new roses seldom thrive in soils where roses have grown before, often succumbing to deficiency diseases (*see p.48*).

FEEDING, WATERING AND MULCHING

A fertile, well-cultivated, weed-free soil is the key to healthy and productive roses. Ideally, prepare it well about three months before planting. Roses prefer a slightly acidic, moist, but well-drained soil, at about pH 6.5. You can lower the pH of acidic soils by adding lime, and raise that of alkaline soils with organic matter. Rotted manure or compost can also be used to improve nutrient retention, drainage, and soil moisture. After spring pruning, feed with a rose fertilizer at the recommended rate and mulch with a 2–4in/5–10cm layer of organic matter to retain moisture and

THIRSTY AT FIRST
Water roses regularly until they are fully established; thereafter, they will need only water during prolonged spells of dry weather.

suppress weeds. Avoid giving fertilizer after midsummer since it induces soft growth, which is prone to cold damage. Instead, use a high-potassium fertilizer in early autumn to help mature wood.

LOOKING AFTER ROSES IN CONTAINERS

Patio and miniature roses are ideal for growing in containers, but their restricted root run means that they rely heavily on regular watering and feeding. Choose a pot that is 12–18in/30–45cm in depth for patio roses or 9–14in/23–35cm for miniature roses. Before planting up, place a piece of mesh over the drainage hole in the bottom. Raise the pot above the ground, using "feet" for example. Fill with a good-quality, soil-based potting mix, since this gives weight for stability, retains nutrients, and is less susceptible to drying out than a peat-based equivalent. Plant the rose in the same way and at the same depth as roses in open ground, but leave about 1in/2.5cm between the soil surface and pot rim to allow for watering. Top-dress with balanced fertilizer after pruning in spring and apply a foliar or liquid fertilizer during the growing season – but don't feed later than midsummer. Check the plant daily for problems, and water thoroughly if the soil mix is dry.

CONTAINER ROSE

Soil surface 1in/2.5cm below rim allows for watering

REMOVING ROSE SUCKERS

Most roses are bud-grafted onto specially selected rootstocks belonging to a different, (usually more vigorous) species. This means that when shoots or "suckers" grow from the roots, they are likely to be stronger than those of the grafted cultivar and may eventually become dominant if they are not removed promptly. Suckers usually arise some distance from the base of the rose and can be clearly identified by their leaf form and color, which differ markedly from that of the grafted rose. Before you remove a sucker, protect your hands with thick, thornproof gloves so that you can grasp it firmly, and make sure that you trace the sucker right back to its point of origin, scraping soil gently away from the roots to do so. Cutting off the sucker at ground level often leaves it with dormant buds that will be stimulated into growth.

1 **Trace the sucker** back to its point of origin on the stem base or root below the graft union, and scrape away the soil carefully by hand or with a trowel.

2 **Grasp the sucker** firmly and pull it away with a sharp and determined tug; this may not be as easy as cutting, but it is far less likely to result in sucker regrowth.

TYING IN CLIMBING AND RAMBLING ROSES

In the wild, roses are held in place by their hooked thorns as they scramble through host plants. When grown on more formal supports, however, climbers and ramblers need to be tied in regularly as their growth extends. When tying onto wires, use rose ties or soft twine in a figure-eight configuration; this is loose enough to allow the stems to expand and buffers them against rubbing or chafing by the wires. On tripods, attach a series of horizontal wires and tie in stems at intervals so that they grow in a spiral fashion around the support. On ropes or chains, guide stems around the support while they are still young and flexible, and secure them at regular intervals with soft twine.

TYING ONTO WIRE   TYING TO A TRIPOD

GUIDING SHOOTS ALONG A ROPE SWAG

ROUTINE PRUNING

R OSES MAY NEED PRUNING for health at any time (*see facing page*), and all types benefit from annual or seasonal pruning to a greater or lesser degree (*see pp.38–45*). Always make clean, correct cuts (*see below*) and use the right tool for the job; use pruners for shoots of ½in/1cm or less in diameter, loppers for shoots up to about 1in/2.5cm across, and a pruning saw for anything bigger.

CUTTING ROSE STEMS

To achieve the ideal cut, aim to make an incision about ¼in/5mm above a bud, angled slightly with the lower end of the cut just opposite the bud so that water is shed away from the bud rather than onto it. The thin blade of your pruners is the cutting blade, so keep this edge nearer to the bud to which you are cutting; otherwise, you crush the stem, leaving a jagged injury that is open to infection.

CUTTING CLEANLY
The correct way to make a cut applies to removing dead wood, deadheading, and all annual pruning. Cuts must be clean, so keep your pruners sharp. If you happen to snag a stem or make the cut too close to the bud, cut back the shoot to the next sound, healthy bud.

Correctly angled cut ¼in/5mm above a bud

CORRECT CUT

Bruised tissue is slow to heal

ROUGH CUT

Cut slopes toward not away from bud

BADLY ANGLED

Too high above the bud

TOO HIGH

DAMAGING CUTS
A rough cut that crushes the stem allows disease to enter. A badly angled cut sheds water onto the bud. Too high a cut leads to stem dieback from the stub.

Narrow cutting blade next to bud

Healthy bud in leaf axil

Stem fits into lopper's bite without straining

CUTTING WITH PRUNERS
Always make cuts to a healthy bud facing in the desired direction of growth. Use pruners for stems of ½in/1cm or less; thicker stems strain the tool and will be bruised or crushed.

USING LOPPERS
Choose loppers to cut large stems; make sure that the stem fits comfortably within the bite of the loppers without straining. For extra leverage, use a pair with long handles.

Removing Dead, Diseased, and Damaged Stems

Cut out dead, diseased, and damaged stems as soon as you notice them throughout the growing season as well as during pruning in the dormant season. Although the best time to remove crossing shoots is in the dormant season, if they rub and chafe other stems they will cause the sort of damage that allows disease-bearing organisms easy access. Since small, clean cuts heal more rapidly than chafing wounds, it is safer to remedy crossing stems in the growing season by cutting to a bud that is facing in a better direction.

With roses, wood that has been dead for some time is usually isolated by the plant's own natural protective barriers, leaving a clear demarcation line between living and dead tissue. Where possible, always make a cut just above the living wood; otherwise, cut to a healthy bud or shoot. Sometimes, however, stem death is caused by a progressive condition known as dieback, which travels back down the stem, staining the inner tissue brown.

White pith indicates healthy wood

REMOVING DIEBACK
Light brown, dried-up stems with no clear line between live and dead tissue probably indicate dieback. To remove the disease, pruning cuts need to be made below the affected portion, so keep cutting back as far as necessary to buds farther down the stem until you reach healthy white pith.

How to Deadhead Roses

Deadheading roses on a warm, dry evening in summer is one of the most therapeutic of tasks, but if it is to benefit the rose as much as the pruner it must be done correctly. The three main purposes are to improve appearances, to prevent the plant using up its energy in setting seed, and, in repeat-flowering roses, to encourage further flushes of good-quality flowers. Never remove just the flowered head, but cut back to a full-size leaf that is facing outward from the center of the plant.

FLORIBUNDA ROSES
Prune out the entire cluster of flowers, making a correctly angled cut to a healthy bud farther down the stem. You can pinch out the central flower that fades first.

HYBRID TEAS AND GRANDIFLORAS
Cut the faded flower back to a healthy bud or sideshoot that is farther down the stem to encourage the production of more flowering shoots later in the season.

PRUNING MODERN BUSH ROSES

T HE MODERN BUSH ROSES INCLUDE the hybrid teas and floribundas as well as their smaller counterparts, the patio, miniature, and groundcover roses, which have relatively minimal pruning needs. Nearly all of the roses in these groups are repeat-flowering, with some of them blooming almost continuously in summer and well into autumn. They bloom most freely on young growth, and, with the exception of groundcover roses, they are best pruned annually in the dormant season to prevent the base of the bush from becoming bare and to create a strong, low framework from which sturdy flowering shoots arise.

PRUNING HYBRID TEAS AND GRANDIFLORAS

Hybrid tea roses should be pruned hard at planting or in their first dormant season (*see p.30*) to within 3–6in/8–15cm of ground level. Cut back strong shoots to an outward-facing bud so that new shoots grow out evenly around an open center. During the growing season, remove diseased, dead, damaged, and crossing shoots, cut out suckers, and deadhead faded flowers as necessary (*see p.37*).

When pruning in the dormant season, cut out all unproductive and unhealthy growth and shorten stems to re-create an open, shapely bush. This stops the bush from becoming bare, resulting in few flowers at the tips of leggy stems. It also helps prevent the buildup of dead wood and keeps an open center through which light and air can penetrate freely, thus reducing the severity of fungal diseases.

HYBRID TEA
Prune when dormant between autumn and early spring. In cold climates, delay until spring as late as possible to avoid cold damage.

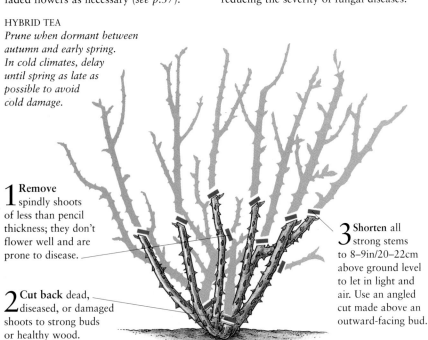

1 Remove spindly shoots of less than pencil thickness; they don't flower well and are prone to disease.

2 Cut back dead, diseased, or damaged shoots to strong buds or healthy wood.

3 Shorten all strong stems to 8–9in/20–22cm above ground level to let in light and air. Use an angled cut made above an outward-facing bud.

PRUNING FOR WINTER PROTECTION

Where winters are cold, delay pruning dormant roses until spring. However, any long shoots remaining on the bush during winter may cause wind resistance, increasing the risk of physical damage from wind-rock. This rocking motion caused by wind loosens roots and creates a gap between roots and soil at ground level. If water enters the gap and freezes it can cause irreparable damage to the graft union – the most vulnerable part of the plant. To prevent this, shorten long shoots by one-third to half of their length in autumn. After any strong winds, check the bush and refirm the soil at the base if necessary.

Shortened stems reduce wind resistance

Tall, whippy shoots

BEFORE PRUNING   AFTER PRUNING

PRUNING FLORIBUNDAS

Floribunda roses are pruned in the same way and at the same time as hybrid teas but not as hard. The effect of massed clusters of small flowers is the greatest part of their charm, so aim to keep long lengths of shoot bearing plenty of buds; from each bud a potential flowering shoot grows. When deadheading large trusses of flowers from floribundas, it is sometimes difficult to find a suitable bud to which to cut. In this case, cut back the stems to the desired height; this usually stimulates a dormant bud into life, and any unwanted stubs can be removed from the plant later.

FLORIBUNDA
Prune hard at planting or in their first dormant season, as for hybrid tea roses, to outward-facing buds 3–6in/8–15cm above ground level. When the rose is established, prune less severely to ensure a long succession of flowers.

3 **Keep the bush open** by cutting back the remaining stems to 10–12in/ 25–30cm above ground level.

1 **Remove** any stems that are crossing or likely to rub against each other at the base.

2 **Cut back** all dead, diseased, and damaged shoots to the base.

4 **Shorten** any sideshoots (laterals) to two or three buds from the main stem, making the cut to an outward-facing bud.

PRUNING PATIO AND MINIATURE ROSES

Patio roses are essentially dwarf versions of floribunda roses, so the timing and technique of pruning is the same as for their larger counterparts – but not so hard. Deadhead them during summer and prune annually when dormant. The miniatures, mostly small-flowered counterparts of larger

bush roses, should be pruned hard at planting, to 2–3in/5–8cm above soil level. If they are growing and flowering well, they need only light pruning. If you notice, though, that the rose is not growing well, prune it hard. Remove all but the strongest stems and shorten these drastically by two-thirds.

MINIATURE ROSES
Since bush size varies, precise prescriptions as to the height of cut are difficult; as a rule, reducing the bush by about one-third will be satisfactory.

2 Tip-prune the main stems, making sure that you also remove the last of the season's faded flowers.

1 Cut out the oldest stems entirely on congested bushes, and remove dead, diseased, damaged, and crossing wood.

3 Prune back any sideshoots to within two or three buds of a main stem to reduce congestion and to stimulate flower-bud production for next year.

PRUNING GROUNDCOVER ROSES

Shrubby groundcover roses need only routine removal of dead wood and deadheading. A little tip-pruning of overlong stems and shortening of laterals may be needed to open up the center of the bush. For rambler types, peg down or cut back overlong stems (*below and right*) depending on how much room is available.

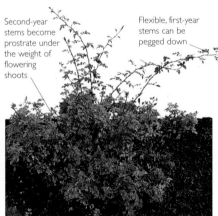

Second-year stems become prostrate under the weight of flowering shoots

Flexible, first-year stems can be pegged down

PEGGING DOWN
The flexible, rooting stems of rambler-type groundcover roses can be pegged down to increase flowering potential and extend cover.

LONG, RAMBLER-TYPE STEMS
Little pruning is necessary, other than to keep the plant within bounds; cut back overlong shoots to an upward-facing bud or shoot.

PRUNING STANDARD ROSES

The aim of pruning a standard rose is to produce a balanced, open head on a clear stem. The height of the stem will vary, from 20in/50cm for patios and miniatures, 30in/75cm for half-standards, to 3½ft/1.1m for full standards; weeping standards are the tallest of all (5–6ft/1.5–2m). Prune the head according to the group of rose grafted on the top of the stem; try to imagine that you are pruning, for example, a hybrid tea and pretend that the graft union is at ground level. Prune repeat-flowering roses during the dormant season; once-flowering roses after flowering.

Pinch shoot between thumb and forefinger

SUCKERS ON STANDARD STEMS
Throughout the growing season, check for and remove any suckers that appear on the clear stem by pinching them out.

Cut back sideshoots to two or three buds

Harder pruning on this side to promote balanced head

Main stems cut back to 20cm above graft union

BEFORE PRUNING
The framework has been shortened in autumn to prevent winter damage. In late winter or early spring, prune to restore a balanced head and to encourage new flowering growth.

AFTER PRUNING
Dead, crossing, and unproductive old wood has been removed. Remaining stems are shortened to about 8in/20cm from the graft union, and laterals shortened to 2–3 buds.

TRIMMING WEEPING STANDARDS

Weeping standards may be created using ramblers, lax climbers, or trailing groundcover roses. Do not prune them for the first couple of years, but remove any dead, diseased, or damaged shoots and shorten spindly shoots to strong buds. Once they are established, they can be pruned according to the rose type. Vigorous ramblers often produce so many new stems that all flowered shoots can be removed each year, cutting back to new basal shoots. On less vigorous ones, prune back one in three of the flowered shoots each year, cutting to upward- or outward-facing buds.

SHORTENING STEMS

REMOVING OLD STEMS

PRUNING SHRUB ROSES

THE SHRUB ROSES include the species, old garden roses, and modern shrubs, and, unlike modern bush roses, most flower on old wood. They are best allowed to develop their full grace and stature with light annual pruning to keep them shapely and to maintain a balance between old wood and vigorous new growth. Exact requirements depend on the growth and flowering habit of an individual cultivar, but, in general, those that flower once are pruned after flowering, while those that repeat are pruned when dormant.

PRUNING OLD GARDEN ROSES

Old roses are pruned lightly at planting; tip-prune any overlong stems and remove damaged or dead shoots. Established roses are pruned in one of two ways (see box, opposite): prune dense growers as you would gallicas (below), removing one or two of the oldest stems each year and shortening the sideshoots close to a main stem to reduce congestion. Others are pruned like albas, which have more spreading growth.

ESTABLISHED GALLICA ROSE
After flowering, prune to reduce crowding and cut out all dead, diseased, damaged, and crossing shoots. In autumn, long whippy stems that extend beyond the main outline can be shortened so that they are not damaged by winter winds.

3 **Shorten** sideshoots by about one-third of their length, cutting back to a strong, healthy, outward-facing bud.

2 **Keep** the rose healthy by removing all dead, damaged, or weak stems, as well as any rubbing against another stem.

1 **Cut out** one or two old, woody stems at the base.

THE DIFFERENT SHRUB ROSE GROUPS

• Alba roses are treated in a similar way to gallicas (*see left, below*), but because they are less dense, you rarely need to cut out entire main stems. Prune after flowering by reducing main shoots to one-third of their length and sideshoots by about two-thirds. Shorten any overlong stems by about one-third in autumn (*see p.39*), cutting to upward-growing shoots.

• Damask, centifolia, and moss roses are all pruned in the same way as alba roses. Hedge plants can be trimmed lightly in winter, but don't attempt to shape them formally.

• Bourbon, China, and Portland roses are treated like albas, but they are repeat-flowering, so pruning is done during the dormant season.

• Hybrid musks are vigorous leafy shrubs that flower repeatedly in summer. In the dormant season, take out one in three of the oldest, unproductive stems, shorten the remainder by up to one-third, then shorten laterals by half.

• Rugosa roses are repeat-flowering and also bear ornamental hips. Prune them during winter by tipping back long stems and taking out old stems occasionally.

PRUNING MODERN SHRUB ROSES

Many modern shrubs can be pruned lightly as shown here; some are large versions of floribunda roses and are pruned similarly (*see p.39*), reducing main stems by one-third and laterals by two-thirds for a compact habit and more flowerbuds.

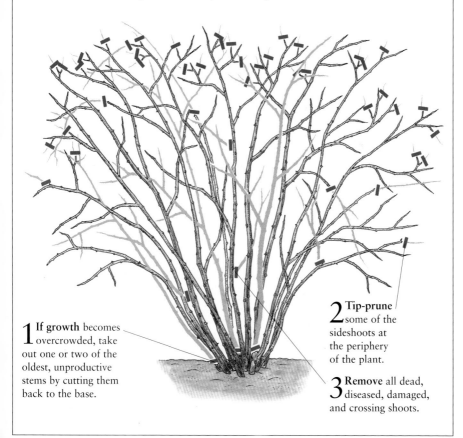

1 **If growth** becomes overcrowded, take out one or two of the oldest, unproductive stems by cutting them back to the base.

2 **Tip-prune** some of the sideshoots at the periphery of the plant.

3 **Remove** all dead, diseased, damaged, and crossing shoots.

PRUNING CLIMBERS AND RAMBLERS

CLIMBERS AND RAMBLERS can be trained in a variety of ways but are most often grown on vertical walls or fences. Here, they need the strong support of horizontal wires set at least 2in/5cm away from the vertical surface to let air circulate freely. Careful training that permits relatively easy access to all parts of the rose will make it much easier to release and adjust ties when pruning, especially when removing entire main stems – this is occasionally necessary for climbers but a regular requirement when pruning ramblers.

PRUNING CLIMBING ROSES

Climbers are mainly repeat-flowering and are pruned when dormant. Don't prune hard at planting: just remove damaged or dead wood and weak shoots. If, once growth begins, the plant is slow to branch, tip-prune main stems by 2–3in/5–8cm,

cutting to a strong bud; this will stimulate laterals to break. Fan out main stems as nearly horizontal as you can, and tie them in at even spacings as they grow. Aim to cover the lower parts of the wall well; gaps will be difficult to fill later on.

PRUNING AN
ESTABLISHED CLIMBER
If possible, prune early in dormancy in autumn to reduce the risk of long stems being whipped about in winter winds. Walls give more protection than is afforded to plants in the open, so pruning can often be delayed until spring.

1 Prune flowered shoots by two-thirds of their length, making angled cuts just above a healthy shoot or bud.

2 Check ties and loosen any that constrict stems. Reposition or shorten any shoots that cross or rub against each other.

3 Where an old stem has ceased to flower well, cut it back to a low bud or shoot.

4 Remove completely any diseased, damaged, or dead wood, along with spindly and leafless growth.

PRUNING RAMBLERS

Ramblers produce new stems from their base each year and flower most freely on wood grown in the previous season, so the techniques and timing for pruning differ from those used for climbers. Ramblers usually flower once in summer and are pruned just after flowering. Prune them hard at planting to about 15in/40cm above ground level to encourage strong shoots. The stems are flexible, so fanning them out to the horizontal to cover an allotted space is easier than it is for climbers. When routinely pruning an established plant, aim to take out about one in three old flowered stems, to encourage replacement shoots. If you wish, you can cut back all flowered stems, but this reduces the plant's stature and, in any case, plants flower perfectly well on the same wood for several years.

OUT-OF-REACH ROSES

Left to their own devices, climbers and ramblers grow steadily upward toward maximum sunlight, producing flowers only at the top of the stems. If you train and prune correctly from the start, the problem is avoided. But if you inherit a neglected specimen, it may be brought back into production by drastic renovation. For ramblers, cut all stems down to the base and wait a season for flowers, or cut out old, moribund stems and leave 3–4 young ones, cutting back their sideshoots by 3–4in/ 8–10cm. For climbers, cut back a proportion of the main stems (1 in 3) to within 12in/30cm of ground level. If the plant is capable of doing so, it produces new stems low down that can be tied in to the support. Some cultivars are reluctant to respond and for these, disguising bare bases with other plants is probably your best option.

PRUNING A RAMBLER
The main aim when pruning established ramblers is to ensure regular replacement of old flowered shoots with new ones that will flower more freely.

1 **Cut back** one in three of the oldest flowered stems to ground level; remove them in sections to avoid tearing the bark of remaining stems.

2 **Shorten** sideshoots from remaining stems by about two-thirds to encourage them to form flowering shoots.

3 **Tip-prune** the main stems by 2–3in/5–8cm to encourage them to produce flowering sideshoots and to keep them in bounds.

4 **Check** ties during the growing season and loosen any that constrict stems. Tie in new stems regularly using a figure-eight tie to allow for stem expansion.

SPECIAL TRAINING FOR ROSES

SOME OF THE most effective forms of special training are produced on vertical features, such as tripods and obelisks. The key to success here depends on applying the principle of training stems to the horizontal. This encourages flowering sideshoots to grow out evenly all along the length of the stems rather than in a cluster at the top of the structure, as they would if left to their own devices. For the best results, use roses with flexible stems.

TRAINING ROSES ON A TRIPOD

Plant a flexible-stemmed rose about 10in/25cm from the base of each tripod leg. Climbers and shrub roses need pruning at planting; cut back ramblers to about 16in/40cm above ground to stimulate strong new shoots. Tie in the stems as they grow, winding them in a spiral around the support to as near horizontal as possible. You will find subsequent pruning easier if you can arrange the stems parallel to each other; any formality will be disguised by leaf growth.

PRUNING A TRIPOD ROSE
For established climbers, maintain a permanent framework of main stems and cut back flowered sideshoots to an outward-facing bud in autumn. For established ramblers, cut back flowered sideshoots by two-thirds and tip-prune main stems after flowering. Remove one or two main stems each year.

1 **Cut back** flowered shoots and any new long shoots not needed for tying in, to maintain the tripod's outline.

2 **Shorten** some older stems to strong young replacement shoots low down, and tie these in where necessary. If cut out in sections, stems are easier to remove and cause least damage to remaining shoots.

3 **Tie in** new stems that grow from the base, winding them carefully toward the horizontal in spiral fashion. Where possible, use them to fill in any low-down gaps as you go.

Pruning Rose Swags

For swags and catenaries (swags in double rows), you need strong, upright pillars 6–8ft/2–2.5m tall and a length of thick ship's rope about 4–5ft/1.2–1.5m longer than the distance between the posts. This allows for a 2ft/60cm dip between them and brings blooms to eye level. Plant one rose 12in/30cm from the base of each post.

Train them straight up the post and then along the rope. On single swags, train two roses to meet midway; for catenaries, train all the roses in the same direction except the one on the last post, where the shoots are trained to meet the preceding rose. Each year, prune out flowered stems and tie in new growth to keep the shape (*below*).

1 **Before pruning,** identify any vigorous new shoots that have grown upward, spoiling the line of the swag. If these shoots are tied down without removing other stems, growth quickly becomes overcongested.

2 **Wearing thick gloves** and safety goggles to protect you against thorns, carefully detach rose stems from the rope and unwind them so that each stem and its sideshoots can be clearly distinguished from the others.

3 **Prune back each** of the flowered main stems to a strong, new shoot. Aim to create an L-shape in the direction of growth. Stems growing in the same direction as the rope will be much easier to tie in.

4 **Taking care** not to damage growth at the junction between the sideshoots and the main stem, straighten the L-shaped stems and wind them around the rope, tying them at intervals with soft twine in a figure-eight.

KEEPING ROSES HEALTHY

ONE OF THE MOST IMPORTANT ways of ensuring that you have healthy roses is to take good care of the soil in which they grow. Keep the soil well aerated, moisture-retentive but well drained, and adequately fertile by mulching annually with well-rotted organic matter and by applying fertilizer in spring and after the first flush of flowers. This will help your roses grow strongly, be more resistant to diseases, and recover quickly from any pest infestations. Correct pruning to permit good air flow and access of light to all parts, and the removal of damaged, diseased, or dead wood as well as faded blooms to conserve the plant's energy, will put you on the path to success.

AVOIDING PROBLEMS

When you visit rose gardens, you will notice that some roses are more healthy than others, even though they have been raised in identical growing conditions. Some roses, including the albas, the rugosas, most climbers, and many modern shrubs are, quite simply, more disease-resistant than others. Choosing notably healthy roses is your first line of defense. The second is to maintain good hygiene. Always remove and discard diseased material immediately, including any fallen infected leaves that harbor fungal spores. Bear in mind that good air circulation is anathema to many fungal infections. The third is to create conditions that deter the proliferation of pests and diseases. You can stem population growth of insect pests by encouraging beneficial insects in your garden; ladybugs, syrphid flies, and predatory wasps consume aphids. Before you reach for the sprayer, make every effort to distinguish between friend and foe.

LADYBUG

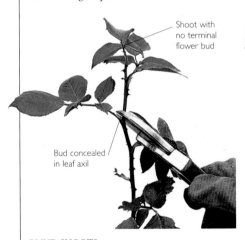

BLIND SHOOTS
Nonflowering shoots often grow from damaged shoot tips. Prune to a bud in the axil of a healthy leaf for a new flowering shoot.

Shoot with no terminal flower bud

Bud concealed in leaf axil

DISEASE-RESISTANT ROSES

Alexander	Just Joey
Anna Ford	Kent
Carefree Beauty	Little Bo-peep
Carefree Delight	Lovely Lady
Carefree Wonder	Mary Rose
Escapade *(cluster-flowered, rose-violet)*	'Nozomi'
	Popcorn
Flower Carpet	Rose Gaujard *(large-flowered, carmine)*
Francine Austin *(cluster-flowered, pure white)*	Sheila's Perfume
	Suma *(ground-cover, deep pink)*
Freedom	
'Fru Dagmar Hastrup'	Sweet Dream
Hertfordshire	Tequila Sunrise
Indian Summer	'The Fairy'
Ingrid Bergman	The Lady *(large-flowered, yellow)*

DAMAGE LIMITATION

It is almost inevitable – in some seasons more so than others – that roses attract one or other of the most common problems (*see below*). Damage limitation relies on rapid action; if you treat as soon as seen, you reduce the risk of pest proliferation and avoid the spread of diseases, which attack soft tissues first. If you do lose roses to disease, weeding will remove any "reservoirs" of problems and help avert rose sickness, where new plantings fail to thrive for no obvious reason – affected roses may recover if replanted elsewhere. Always weed by hand around the root zone of roses to avoid incurring any damage to fragile feeder roots.

USING PESTICIDES

If used appropriately, most pesticides present few problems to the environment and are certainly effective in controlling pests and diseases, but always assess whether the problem really justifies their use. Any slight infestations may be dealt with by nipping off affected parts, or even by squashing pests by hand. If possible, use a pest-specific chemical that, for example, kills only aphids. The use of a combined insecticide and fungicide is justifiable only when both problems are present at levels that warrant control. Having made sure that the chemical fits the need, follow the manufacturers' instructions as to timing, application rate, and frequency of use. Applications are best made at dusk, when most beneficial insects have stopped flying.

APHIDS
Present from midspring onward. Treat before heavy infestation develops; pick off or spray with water.

SAWFLY DAMAGE
Rolled leaflets in late spring to early summer; harmless but ugly. Pick off light infestations or use systemic insecticide.

BLACKSPOT
Purple-black spots, yellowing, and leaf drop; use systemic fungicide after spring pruning; repeat as advised on the label.

POWDERY MILDEW
Cut out and discard leaves with powdery white bloom; use systemic fungicide. Keep well mulched and watered.

ROSE LEAFHOPPERS
Leaf speckling in summer; tiny, pale yellow, sapsucking insects beneath. Control with a systemic insecticide.

ROSE BALLING
Prevalent in wet weather; not immediately harmful, but prune out before blooms go moldy and admit dieback.

DISPLAYING ROSES

ROSES MAKE LOVELY CUT FLOWERS, and a little care *(see below)* helps prolong their beauty. Showing your roses can be a most satisfying, although challenging and very competitive, activity. Standards of cultivation are impeccable at shows, and rules for exhibiting are detailed and strict. If you are bitten by the bug and have the time to devote to growing for exhibition, your first step should be to join your local or national rose society where you can enjoy access to a wealth of knowledge and experience.

SHOWING TECHNIQUES

Exhibition roses are usually grown on groups of three or more plants to permit selection of perfect blooms. Plants are pruned to a limited number of shoots and fed heavily to yield only a few flowers per year; flowers are disbudded to produce quality blooms. There are also precise rules to which you need to conform when staging roses; for example, a hybrid tea must be three-quarters open at judging, while floribunda roses have blooms in a cycle of openness but without any fading of the stamens. Even when you have the perfect blooms, you must conform to show schedules to avoid disqualification.

DISBUDDING HYBRID TEA ROSES
Remove newly formed sidebuds so that the main bud develops strongly.

DISBUDDING FLORIBUNDA ROSES
Pinch out the central bud of a cluster so other blooms open at the same time.

CARING FOR CUT FLOWERS

Nearly all roses are suitable for cutting, but they usually need the support of florists' foam or a scrunch of wire netting. Cut roses early in the day when the blooms are about three-quarters open – try to cut about 12in/30cm of stem. Remove thorns and some of the lower leaves, then plunge them to their necks in warm, fresh water for a few hours before arranging. Cut roses last longer if you slant the cut across the stems while still submerged. Change the water every two or three days and use a commercial cut flower food. Roses mix well with the formal spires of delphiniums and airy panicles of baby's breath, or with cornflower or larkspur. For foliage contrast, use silver artemisia, ferns, or dark-leaved *Cotinus*.

WILD BEAUTY
Even species roses can be used as cut flowers; they are especially effective in naturalistic arrangements. For foliage interest, use the ferny-leaved R. pimpinellifolia, *the gray-leaved* R. glauca, *or* R. rugosa *(above).*

A CALENDAR OF ROSE CARE

SPRING

• Plant new container-grown roses and complete plantings of bare-root roses. Heel in bare-root roses and keep container-grown ones well-watered if planting is delayed. Soak well before and after planting.

• Prune newly planted modern bush and standard roses, and other repeat-flowering roses, in early spring.

• When soil is thoroughly moist, apply fertilizer to the base of established plants and water it in; mulch with well-rotted organic matter.

• Repot roses grown in containers and apply a top-dressing.

• Start checking for pest and disease infestations (see p.49) and treat immediately.

• Check for and remove suckers.

SUMMER

• Plant newly acquired container-grown roses, but not in prolonged spells of dry weather. Water until well established.

• Thin gallicas, and prune once-flowering roses after flowering.

• Deadhead repeat-flowering roses and others not grown for ornamental hips; give a second application of fertilizer after the first flush of flowers.

• Water established, open-ground roses in prolonged drought, and roses in pots each or every other day, as necessary.

• Maintain weed control throughout the growing season.

• Check regularly and treat pests and diseases, if necessary, as soon as seen.

• Train and tie in strong new shoots of climbers throughout the growing season.

• Peruse mail-order catalogs and order for new plantings in autumn.

AUTUMN

• Prepare soil for new plantings; cultivate deeply and incorporate well-rotted organic matter.

• Shorten long shoots of climbers and begin pruning bush roses in mild-winter regions.

• Trim back long stems on bush and shrub roses to reduce wind-rock in winter.

• Trim roses grown as informal hedging; delay pruning plants with a display of hips until late winter.

• Begin planting bare-root roses in spells of fine weather if soil is moist and workable. If weather is poor, heel them in and keep roots moist until conditions improve.

• Cut back any summer-flowering companion perennials; divide and replant if necessary.

• Gather and discard dead wood, fallen leaves, and other debris, especially that affected by disease.

WINTER

• Continue to plant in spells of mild weather when soil is not wet or frozen. If planting of container-grown roses is delayed, protect pot and roots from cold.

• Move any young roses that you have sited badly, but do not replant in soil that roses have grown in before.

• Check regularly for soil heave on unmulched plants, and refirm soil around the roots if possible.

• In cold winters, mound soil over crowns; in very harsh winters, use a deep, dry mulch of straw or leaves, held in place with netting or similar. In severe conditions, lift and bury roses on their sides in a deep, straw-lined trench and cover with 12in/30cm of soil.

• Renovate old, neglected roses of all types.

VACATION WATERING
A full bucket of water with a "wick" of fabric pushed into the soil mix gives roses in pots access to water while you are away.

MOUNDING SOIL
In areas where winter temperatures are likely to fall below -14°F/-10°C, mound soil over the crown of each rose plant to a minimum depth of 6in/12cm in late autumn. This protects the vulnerable graft union from becoming frozen.

A GALLERY OF ROSES

THE ROSES DESCRIBED HERE are suitable for most of North America if given appropriate care and they are reasonably resistant to disease. The selection represents a small fraction of roses offered by nurseries, garden centers and mail-order businesses. Roses are grouped by flower form, size, and habit.

HYBRID TEA ROSES

Pristine
Scented, high-pointed
flowers. To 4ft/1.2m.

ALSO KNOWN AS LARGE-FLOWERED bush roses, these have a bushy or upright habit and bear large, usually many-petaled, often fragrant flowers, singly or in small clusters. Most flower from summer to autumn, either continuously or in successive flushes. They are traditionally pruned back hard every year (*see p.38*) for the finest flowers; regular deadheading (*see p.37*) promotes repeat blooming. Ideal as cut flowers, and most, especially those of upright habit, look their best in formal rose beds. Use those of bushy habit and thorny growth as a hedge.

Polar Star
Dark glossy leaves and
perfect, creamy white, lightly
scented flowers. To 3ft/1m.

Warm Wishes
Dark leaves and peach-pink
blooms with a strong, sweet
scent. To 3½ft/1.1m.

Paul Shirville
Dark glossy leaves, fragrant,
high-pointed blooms, and a
spreading habit. To 3ft/1m.

◀ OLD BEAUTY *Purplish leaves offset the bright pink blooms of the species rose* R. glauca.

Lovely Lady
Fragrant, pointed, salmon-pink blooms and glossy leaves. To 2½ft/75cm.

Double Delight
Sweetly scented, rounded blooms of creamy yellow flushed carmine. To 3ft/1m.

Elina
Dark, red-tinted leaves and ivory flowers with yellow centers. To 3½ ft/1.1m.

Rosemary Harkness
Glossy, dark leaves, with sweet-scented apricot to salmon flowers. To 2½ft/80cm.

Fragrant Cloud
Free-flowering, with large, strongly fragrant, dusky scarlet blooms. To 2½ft/75cm.

Just Joey
Large, fragrant, perfectly
shaped, coppery pink flowers
during summer. To 2½ft/75cm.

Tequila Sunrise
Scarlet-margined, rich yellow,
lightly scented flowers and
an open habit. To 2½ft/75cm.

Valencia
Large, high-centered, strongly
fragrant flowers of a rich
amber-yellow. To 2½ft/75cm.

MORE CHOICES

'Lover's Meeting'
Bronzed leaves and high-
centered, fragrant, reddish
orange flowers. To 2½ft/75cm.

FOR FRAGRANCE
Alec's Red Deep crimson
to cherry red
Big Purple Beet purple
Broadway Orange-yellow
'Chrysler Imperial' Deep red
Dolly Parton Large orange-red
Indian Summer Creamy
orange
Mister Lincoln Dark red
Paradise Red-tipped lavender
Pot o'Gold Golden yellow
Whisky Mac Pale amber-
yellow

FOR COLOR
Alexander Vermilion red
Dainty Bess Single, pink
with maroon stamens
First Prize Two-tone pink
Freedom Rich bright yellow
Ingrid Bergman Dark red
Olympiad Bright red
Pascali Pure white
Peace Yellow, flushed
pink
Remember Me Copper
Touch of Class White,
blushed pink

FLORIBUNDA AND GRANDIFLORA ROSES

ALSO KNOWN AS CLUSTER-FLOWERED bush roses, these have an upright or bushy habit and produce their often fragrant, single or double flowers in clusters of 3–25. Most flower repeatedly, almost continuously through summer and early autumn. Deadheading (*see p.37*) encourages plentiful blooms; during the dormant period, they should be pruned hard (*see p.39*). Many are useful as cut flowers and are suitable as hedging and in borders. Slightly more graceful in habit than the hybrid teas, they mix well with other shrubs in a mixed border.

Intrigue
Purple-green leaves and dark red flowers. To 2½ft/75cm.

Jacqueline du Pré
Musk-scented, semidouble, ivory-white flowers. Suitable for hedging. To 5ft/1.5m.

'English Miss'
Camellia-like blooms. Easy to grow and good for hedging. To 2½ft/75cm.

'The Queen Elizabeth'
Dark, glossy leaves and pink flowers. Ideal for cutting and mixed borders. To 7ft/2.2m.

Escapade
Fragrant, white-eyed blooms.
Good for cutting and mixed
borders. To 2½ft/75cm.

Sheila's Perfume
Fragrant yellow flowers edged
with red. Use for cutting and
hedging. To 2½ft/75cm.

Trumpeter
Large, bright orange-red
flowers, good for containers
and low hedges. To 2ft/75cm.

'Korresia'
Fragrant, rich flowers and
light foliage for borders and
cut flowers. To 2½ft/75cm.

'Oranges and Lemons'
Scarlet-striped, orange-yellow
blooms and dark leaves; good
for borders. To 2½ft/75cm.

MORE CHOICES

Amber Queen Scented,
   amber-yellow
Angel Face Deep mauve,
   fragrant
Cherish Light pink
Ferdy Rich coral-pink
Gold Medal Deep yellow
Iceberg Creamy white
Impatient Bright orange-red
Love Red petals with white
   undersides
Mountbatten Yellow
Sexy Rexy Rose-pink
'Southampton' Apricot

PATIO AND MINIATURE ROSES

Robin Redbreast
Single, white-centered, dark red blooms. To 18in/45cm.

Patio roses are dwarf versions of floribunda roses and, like them, bear single to double, usually unscented flowers, in clusters throughout the summer. They are perfect for small gardens, as low bedding or in formal borders, and are ideal for growing in containers to decorate a patio or paved area. Miniature roses are similar but even smaller bushes, which also bloom in succession throughout summer. They are superb for containers, confined spaces, and edging paths or borders. They can be kept in shape with minimal pruning (*see p.40*).

'White Pet'
Profuse clusters of white, rosette-form flowers. Deep pink in bud. To 18in/45cm.

Queen Mother
Dark green leaves and clusters of semidouble, soft, clear pink blooms. To 16in/40cm.

Baby Masquerade
Clusters of small, rosette-form yellow flowers aging to pink and crimson. To 16in/40cm.

Little Bo-peep
Short-stemmed, semidouble, pale pink flowers and dark, glossy foliage. To 12in/30cm.

'Hula Girl'
Slightly scented, urn-shaped, pale orange-pink flowers and glossy foliage. To 20in/50cm.

Anna Ford
Flat, semidouble, orange-red flowers with a yellow center. Dark leaves. To 18in/45cm.

Orange Sunblaze
Dense, very compact habit
and bright orange-red
blooms. To 12in/30cm.

'Fire Princess'
Rosette-form, bright scarlet
flowers above glossy, dark
green leaves. To 18in/45cm.

Sweet Dream
Fully double, peachy apricot
flowers above midgreen,
matte leaves. To 16in/40cm.

Festival
Crimson-scarlet blooms with
silver tints on the petal
reverse. To 24in/60cm.

Boys' Brigade
Clusters of lightly scented,
tiny flowers, each with a pale
cream eye. To 18in/45cm.

MORE CHOICES

Black Jade Deep red
Cupcake Midpink
'De Meaux' Clear pink
Green Ice Greenish white
Jeanne Lajoie Lavender-
pink
Magic Carrousel Crimson-
edged yellow
Popcorn Vigorous; white
Red Cascade Climbing red
Rise 'n' Shine Yellow
Starina Orange-red
Stars 'n' Stripes White with
red stripes

GROUNDCOVER ROSES

Swany
Spreading, with masses of
double flowers. To 30in/75cm.

Tʜᴇsᴇ ʀᴏsᴇs have a dense, small-leaved habit; some, such as the "County" roses Hertfordshire and Kent, are spreading and arching. Others, such as 'Nozomi', trail along near to the ground, rooting as they go. A few bloom once only, but most flower almost continuously in summer, often crowding the stems with single to double, usually unscented, blooms. Use them to cascade over walls and banks, in beds, and at the front of borders. Prune lightly to keep them neat (*see p.40*). Trouble-free and easy to grow, they are good for containers.

White Flower Carpet
Very dense habit, with glossy
leaves and double, ivory-tinted
white flowers. To 24in/60cm.

Kent
Compact and spreading,
with clusters of semidouble
white flowers. To 18in/45cm.

Pheasant
Low, creeping habit and
abundant clusters of rose-
pink flowers. To 20in/50cm.

Flower Carpet
Dense, spreading habit and
clusters of deep rose-pink
flowers. To 30in/75cm.

Cambridgeshire
Semidouble blooms in
shades of gold, pink, and
scarlet. To 18in/45cm.

Hertfordshire
Dense and free-flowering,
with single, carmine-pink
flowers. To 18in/45cm.

'Nozomi'
Trailing habit, with a single
flush of pale pink flowers
in summer. To 18in/45cm.

MORE CHOICES

"COUNTY" ROSES
Avon White, flushed pale
  pearly pink with golden
  stamens
Berkshire Bright cherry pink,
  with golden stamens
Gwent Lemon-yellow
Northamptonshire Pearly
  white to pink
Suffolk Bright scarlet with
  yellow stamens
Surrey Salmon-pink
Sussex Buff-apricot
Wiltshire Deep reddish pink

OTHERS
Blenheim White
Bonica Rose-pink
Broadlands Sulfur-yellow
Eyeopener Bright red with
  yellow eye
La Sévillana Scarlet
Magic Carpet Lilac-pink
'Max Graf' Pink
Pink Bells Bright pink
Red Blanket Rosy red
Red Trail Bright red
Rosy Cushion Pink
  with white eye

OLD GARDEN AND SPECIES ROSES

'Madame de Sancy
de Parabère'
Summer blooms. To 15ft/5m.

THE OLD ROSES are of European origin and include the oldest cultivated roses; some have been grown for many centuries. Most bloom once – magnificently – in late spring or early summer and are much loved for their divine scents, sumptuous flower form, and soft or rich colors, which often take on distinctive tints as they age. They are perfect for mixed borders and as specimens. The species roses, and named selections of the species, are also mostly once-blooming with single or semidouble flowers. Species roses are ideal for natural-style plantings.

'Boule de Neige'
Fragrant pink buds and white flowers repeating throughout summer. To 5ft/1.5m.

'Dupontii'
Single, scented, creamy white flowers borne in a single flush in summer. To 7ft/2.2m.

'Frau Karl Druschki'
Vigorous, with milky white flowers, repeating throughout summer. To 5ft/1.5m.

'Stanwell Perpetual'
Fragrant, soft pink flowers repeating in flushes during summer. To 3ft/1m.

'Félicité Parmentier'
Fragrant, cream to pale pink flowers borne in a single flush in summer. To 4ft/1.2m.

'Great Maiden's Blush'
Very fragrant, with abundant clear pink flowers in a single flush in summer. To 6½ft/2m.

R. rubiginosa
Apple-scented leaves; pink
blooms borne in a single flush
in summer. To 8ft/2.5m.

R. x *centifolia* 'Muscosa'
Mossy stems and scented,
cupped, pink flowers borne in
a single flush. To 5ft/1.5m.

**R. *gallica* var. *officinalis*
'Versicolor'**
Pale pink, red-striped flowers
in late spring. To 2½ft/80cm.

'Président de Sèze'
Scented, pale lilac-pink
flowers packed with petals
during summer. To 4ft/1.2m.

'Paul Neyron'
Scented flowers of lilac-tinted
pink, repeated in flushes in
summer. To 5ft/1.5m.

'Bourbon Queen'
Fragrant rose-pink flowers,
often repeated in flushes,
in summer. To 8ft/2.5m.

'Salet'
Scented flowers, occasionally repeated in flushes, in summer. To 4ft/1.2m.

'Duc de Guiche'
Rich crimson flowers, scented and packed with petals, borne once in summer. To 4ft/1.2m.

'Geranium'
Single red blooms in summer, followed by flask-shaped scarlet hips. To 8ft/2.5m.

'Empereur du Maroc'
Fragrant deep crimson flowers, may repeat in flushes, in summer. To 4ft/1.2m.

'Baron Girod de l'Ain'
Scented flowers with white-lined petals borne throughout summer. To 4ft/1.2m.

R. moschata
Musk-scented, single white flowers of summer give rise to orange-red hips. To 10ft/3m.

Golden Chersonese
Wreaths of small golden flowers in late spring, above ferny leaves. To 7ft/2.2m.

'Reine des Violettes'
Scented, vibrant violet-purple flowers are borne in repeat flushes in summer. To 7ft/2m.

MORE CHOICES

'Belle de Crécy' Fragrant, deep purple-pink
'Cardinal de Richelieu' Scented, burgundy-purple
'Complicata' Single, pink, pale-centered
'Du Maître de l'Ecole' Purple, aging to lilac-pink
R. glauca Gray-purple foliage and pink flowers
'Madame Hardy' Double white with green eye
'Zéphirine Drouhin' Fragrant, deep pink

SHRUB ROSES

Graham Thomas
Fragrant yellow summer
blooms. Up to 4ft/1.2m.

THE SHRUB ROSES are a diverse group. Generally larger than bush roses and often with thorny stems, they have usually scented flowers, from single to fully double, borne singly or in clusters. Most were bred during this century and have the modern characteristic of flowering repeatedly from summer into autumn. Shrub roses are not as neat as large-flowered bushes and are pruned less rigidly (*see pp.42–3*). They are ideal for mixed borders or as specimens, and many of the robust varieties are good for hedging and barrier plantings.

Many Happy Returns
Scented, semi double, pink
flowers in clusters through
summer. To 30in/75cm.

Constance Spry
Myrrh-scented, fully double,
pink flowers borne in early
to midsummer. To 6½ft/2m.

'Roseraie de l'Haÿ'
Scented, double, magenta
flowers all summer.
To 6½ft/2.2m.

Armada
Scented, semidouble, pink
blooms during summer, and
glossy leaves. To 5ft/1.5m.

Sally Holmes
Large clusters of scented,
single, creamy white flowers
through summer. To 6½ft/2m.

MORE CHOICES

Abraham Darby Scented, apricot-pink
Carefree Beauty Vigorous; semidouble, midpink
Fru Dagman Hastrup Clove–scented, midpink
Gertrude Jekyll Fragrant, rich pink
'Golden Wings' Single, scented, pale yellow
Morden Centennial Double pink, repeats
'The Fairy' Pale pink
Westerland Vigorous, glowing apricot-orange

CLIMBING ROSES

CLIMBING ROSES can be grown on walls, trellises, fences, and pillars. A few bloom only once, but most bear flowers repeatedly in summer. Many are scented, and their colors and flower forms, whether borne singly or in clusters, are diverse. Climbers generally have stiff, upright growth and produce most of their blooms on sideshoots arising from a woody framework. For the best display, train them carefully in the early years (see pp.46–7); otherwise, they grow rapidly upward, bearing blooms out of reach of both eye and nose.

Dublin Bay
Rich red flowers all summer. Up to 7ft/2.2m.

'Mermaid'
Single, cupped, soft yellow flowers with golden stamens, in summer. To 20ft/6m.

Handel
Stiffly upright growth carries creamy white flowers with magenta margins. To 10ft/3m.

'Aloha'
Scented rose-pink and salmon-pink flowers all summer. To 10ft/3m.

Compassion
Fragrant, salmon-pink blooms tinged with apricot produced through summer. To 10ft/3m.

Bantry Bay
Semidouble, pale pink flowers with light scent borne all summer. To 13ft/4m.

Summer Wine
Stiffly upright growth bears single flowers of coral-pink through summer. To 10ft/3m.

Dortmund
Clusters of single, white-eyed red flowers borne freely all summer. To 10ft/3m.

Danse du Feu
Double, rich scarlet flowers in summer, offset against glossy midgreen leaves. To 8ft/2.5m.

Sympathie
Glossy leaves bejewelled with fully double, deep red flowers all summer. To 10ft/3m.

Golden Showers
Fragrant, double, clear yellow blooms borne in clusters all summer. To 10ft/3m.

'Laura Ford' ♀
Upright, with scented, semi-double yellow flowers borne in summer. To 7ft/2.2m.

MORE CHOICES

Altissimo Bright red, single
America Coral–pink, repeats
American Pillar Carmine–red, white eye
Blaze Semidouble red
City of York Creamy white
Climbing Iceberg Creamy white, repeats
Joseph's Coat Yellow aging to orange then red
Sombreuil Creamy white
William Baffin Deep pink, very hardy

RAMBLING ROSES

'Albertine'
Scented pink flowers in
summer. Thorny. To 16ft/5m.

RAMBLERS differ from climbers in that they tend
to produce very long, flexible shoots annually
from the base and bear quite spectacular sprays of
flowers once only in summer. Many are rampant
growers, making them ideal for growing through
old trees or over pergolas that hide unsightly garden
structures; the flexible stems can also be trained to
form swags on ropes. If training on walls, the trellis
must be set away from the wall to let air circulate
freely behind stems; ramblers are prone to powdery
mildew, which thrives in warm, stagnant air.

'Sanders' White Rambler'
Fully double white flowers
borne in large clusters in
late summer. To 13ft/4m.

'New Dawn'
Softest blush pink, double
flowers are produced all
through summer. To 10ft/3m.

'Félicité Perpétue'
Small, fully double, pale
pink flowers are borne freely
during summer. To 16ft/5m.

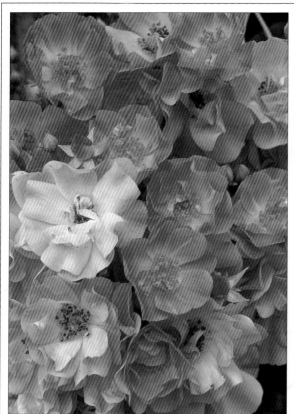

'Blush Rambler'
Dense clusters of semidouble,
pale pink flowers borne
during summer. To 13ft/4m.

'François Juranville'
Apple-scented, rosette-shaped,
scented, salmon-pink flowers
borne in summer. To 20ft/6m.

'Seagull'
Masses of single white
flowers with golden stamens
in summer. To 20ft/6m.

'Crimson Shower'
Cascades of double, crimson
flowers wreathe lax stems all
through summer. To 8ft/2.5m.

'Easlea's Golden Rambler'
Small clusters of scented,
apricot-yellow flowers flecked
red, in summer. To 20ft/6m.

MORE CHOICES

'Adélaïde d'Orléans'
Lightly scented,
semidouble, pale pink

'Bleu Magenta' Double,
deep purple with yellow
stamens

'Paul's Himalayan Musk'
Small, double, lilac-pink,
in large sprays

'Phyllis Bide' Small,
double, buff-pink flushed
yellow, darken with age

'Wedding Day' Fruit-
scented, single, creamy
white ageing to blush pink

INDEX

ACKNOWLEDGMENTS

Picture research Neale Chamberlain,
Sam Ruston

Index Hilary Bird

DK Publishing would also like to thank:
Susanne Mitchell, Karen Wilson and Barbara
Haynes at the RHS, Vincent Square.

American Horticultural Society
Visit AHS at www.ahs.org or call them
at 1-800-777-7931 ext. 10. Membership
benefits include *The American Gardener*
magazine, free admission to flower shows,
the free seed exchange, book services,
and the Gardener's Information Service.

Photography
The publisher would like to thank the
following for their kind permission
to reproduce the photographs:
(key: a=above, b=below, c=centre, l=left,
r=right, t=top)

A-Z Botanical Collection: 66cl. **Neil
Campbell-Sharp:** jacket front clt; 19tr, 20br,
21tr, 57cl, 69bc. **Eric Crichton Photos:** 8b,
16b, 18br, 21tl, 23tr, 24b, 61tl, 65cr.
Garden Picture Library: John Glover 61cl.
John Glover: jacket back ct; 6, 7bl, 9br, 14br,
15t, 26cl, 27t, 52, 59bc. **Jerry Harpur:** 9tl,
14bl, 17tl, 26br. **Andrew Lawson:** jacket front
clb; 18bl, 20bl, 25br. **Clive Nichols:** Wollerton
Old Hall, Shropshire: 24tl. **Photos
Horticultural:** 22br. **Howard Rice:** 2, 10b,
19tl. **Harry Smith Collection:** 13t